GRANNIES

Everyone loves granny squ... ...em
like this before. Crochete... ...ply Soft yarn, these
creations are colorful, comfortable, and so much fun! From a bright
floral wrap to a fringed afghan, the six designs have fresh appeal.
They're absolutely lovely to share as gifts. With the luxurious feel
of Simply Soft, you'll also want to crochet a few for yourself!

eisure Arts, Inc.
ttle Rock, Arkansas

go check on granny

■■■▶ **EXPERIENCED**

designed by Kelly Klem

FINISHED MEASUREMENT
56"/142cm square

MATERIALS
Caron International's Simply Soft **MEDIUM 4**
(100% acrylic; 6 oz/170g, 315 yds/288m):
#9756 Lavender Blue, 21 oz (A)
#9722 Plum Wine, 12 oz (B)
#9705 Sage, 12 oz (C)
Caron International's Simply Soft Brites
(100% acrylic; 6 oz/170g, 315 yds/288m):
#9609 Berry Blue, 6 oz (D)

Crochet hooks, one each size US K/10.5 (6.5mm) (for body), US I/9 (5.5mm) (for final rnd only), or size to obtain gauge.
Yarn needle

GAUGE
Rnds 1-5 = 4" x 4"/10 x 10 cm.
Gauge is not critical for this project.

ABBREVIATIONS

rep	repeat
rnd(s)	round(s)
sk	skip
sp(s)	space(s)
st(s)	stitch(es)

SPECIAL TECHNIQUE

Adjustable-ring method — Wrap yarn into a ring, ensuring that the tail falls behind the working yarn. Between finger and thumb, grip ring and tail firmly. Insert hook through center of ring, yarn over (with working yarn) and draw up a loop. Yarn over and draw through loop on hook (first chain stitch made). Work stitches of first round in the ring. After the second round of stitches is worked, pull gently, but firmly, on tail to tighten ring.

STITCHES USED

Chain (ch)
Double crochet (dc)
Single crochet (sc)
Slip stitch (sl st)
Treble crochet (tr)

NOTES

1. This project uses almost all yardage of all skeins.
2. The afghan is formed from a unique double-layer of fabric, with stitches of both layers interlaced. Each round consists of a back layer and a front layer. The stitches of each round are interlaced by working some of the stitches through both layers of the fabric. The back layer is worked using one color and the front layer may be worked using a different color.
3. Work with **right** side facing throughout.
4. When swapping colors between layers, do **not** fasten off. Follow the instructions at the beginning and end of each round carefully to change colors without the need for fastening off and rejoining.
5. Add new colors (or a new skein) at the beginning of a round, as follows: place loop of old color back on hook, leave a long tail and draw a loop of the new color through the loop of the old color. Gently pull loop of old color tight around loop of new color and fasten off old color leaving a long tail. Work following corner stitches over the tails.

COLOR SEQUENCE

Rnds 1–19, work back layers with A, and front layers with B.

Rnd 20 and Rnd 21 (back layer only), work all layers with A.

Rnd 21 (front layer), Rnds 22–26, and Rnd 27 (back layer only), work back layers with D, and front layers with C.

Rnd 27 (front layer), Rnd 28, and Rnd 29 (back layer only), work all layers with A.

Rnd 29 (front layer), Rnds 30–34, and Rnd 35 (back layer only), work back layers with C, and front layers with B.

Rnd 35 (front layer), Rnds 36–37, work all layers with A.

AFGHAN

With larger hook and A, make an adjustable ring.

Rnd 1 (back layer): Ch 3 (counts as dc here and throughout), work 2 dc in ring, ch 3, [3 dc in ring, ch 3] 3 times; join with sl st in top of beginning ch; sl st in next 2 dc and in first ch-3 sp—Four 3-dc groups and 4 ch-3 sps. Enlarge loop on hook, remove hook from loop, and keep this loop and yarn strand in back while working the next layer. Do **not** fasten off.

Rnd 1 (front layer): Working in front of sts of back layer, draw up a loop of B in the center ring between any two 3-dc groups, ch 3, (tr, dc) in same sp as join (corner made); *working in sts of back layer, sc in next dc, ch 1, dc in next dc, ch 1, sc in next dc; working in front of sts of back layer, (dc, tr, dc) in center ring between next two 3-dc groups (corner made); rep from * 2 more times; working in sts of back layer, sc in next dc, ch 1, dc in next dc, ch 1, sc in next dc; join with sl st in top of beginning ch (of this layer); sl st in next tr—4 corners, 8 sc, 4 dc, and 8 ch-1 sps. Enlarge loop on hook, remove hook from loop, and keep this loop and yarn strand in front while working the next layer. Do **not** fasten off. Pull gently, but firmly on beginning tail to close center ring.

Note: In the next round, some stitches are worked through both layers of fabric. When instructed to work into a stitch of the front layer and corresponding ch-3 sp of the back layer, you should work into both of these stitches at the same time. Insert your hook into the stitch and into the ch-3 sp behind the stitch, then complete the stitch as usual. Here and when working all back layers, unless instructed to work through both layers, all other stitches are worked in the front layer of the previous round.

Rnd 2 (back layer): Place loop of A back on hook, sl st in next dc of front layer and corresponding ch-3 sp of back layer, ch 3, 2 dc in same sp (working through both layers), ch 3, sk next tr (of front layer) , 3 dc in next dc and same corresponding ch-3 sp of back layer (corner made), *sk next sc, sc in next dc, sk next sc, 3 dc in next dc and corresponding ch-3 sp of back layer, ch 3, sk next tr, 3 dc in next dc and same corresponding ch-3 sp of back layer (corner made); rep from * 2 more times, sk next sc, sc in next dc; join with sl st in top of beginning ch (of this layer); sl st in next 2 dc and in first ch-3 sp— 4 corners and 1 sc between each corner. Enlarge loop on hook and keep this loop and yarn strand in back while working the next layer. Do **not** fasten off.

Notes: Take care, when working through both layers to work through the front and back layers of the previous round (not the front layer of the previous round and the back layer of the current round). Here and when working all front layers, unless instructed to work through both layers, all other stitches are worked in the back layer of the previous round.

Rnd 2 (front layer): Place loop of B back on hook, ch 3, (tr, dc) in same tr of front layer and corresponding ch-3 sp of previous back layer, *sc in next dc (of current back layer), ch 1, dc in next dc, ch 1, sc in next dc; sl st in back loop of next sc, sc in next dc, ch 1, dc in next dc, ch 1, sc in next dc; (dc, tr, dc) in next tr of front layer

and corresponding ch-3 sp; rep from * 2 more times, sc in next dc, ch 1, dc in next dc, ch 1, sc in next dc; sl st in back loop of next sc, sc in next dc, ch 1, dc in next dc, ch 1, sc in next dc; join with sl st in top of beginning ch; sl st in next tr. Enlarge loop on hook and keep this loop and yarn strand in front while working the next layer. Do **not** fasten off.

Rnd 3 (back layer): Place loop of A back on hook, sl st in next dc of front layer and corresponding ch-3 sp, ch 3, 2 dc in same sp (working through both layers), ch 3, sk next tr, 3 dc in next dc and same corresponding ch-3 sp, *sk next sc, sc in next dc, sk next sc, 3 dc in free loop of next sc of previous back layer, sk next sc, sc in next dc, sk next sc; 3 dc in next dc and corresponding ch-3 sp, ch 3, sk next tr, 3 dc in next dc and same corresponding ch-3 sp; rep from * 2 more times, sk next sc, sc in next dc, sk next sc, 3 dc in free loop of next sc of previous back layer, sk next sc, sc in next dc; join with sl st in top of beginning ch; sl st in next 2 dc and in first ch-3 sp. Enlarge loop on hook and keep this loop and yarn strand in back while working the next layer. Do **not** fasten off.

Rnd 3 (front layer): Place loop of B back on hook, ch 3, (tr, dc) in same tr of front layer and corresponding ch-3 sp of previous back layer, *sc in next dc (of current back layer), ch 1, dc in next dc, ch 1, sc in next dc; **sl st in back loop of next sc, sc in next dc, ch 1, dc in next dc, ch 1, sc in next dc; rep from ** across to next corner ch-3 sp; (dc, tr, dc) in next tr of front layer and corresponding ch-3 sp; rep from * 2 more times, sc in next dc, ch 1, dc in next dc, ch 1, sc in next dc; ***sl st in back loop of next sc, sc in next dc, ch 1, dc in next dc, ch 1, sc in next dc; rep from *** across to beginning of rnd; join with sl st in top of beginning ch; sl st in next tr. Enlarge loop on hook and keep this loop and yarn strand in front while working the next layer. Do **not** fasten off.

Rnd 4 (back layer): Place loop of A back on hook, sl st in the next dc of front layer and corresponding ch-3 sp, ch 3, 2 dc in same sp (working through both layers), ch 3, sk next tr, 3 dc in next dc and same corresponding ch-3 sp; *sk next sc, sc in next dc, sk next sc, **3 dc in free loop of next sc of previous back layer, sk next sc, sc in next dc, sk next sc; rep from ** across to next corner, 3 dc in next dc and corresponding ch-3 sp, ch 3, sk next tr, 3 dc in next dc and same corresponding ch-3 sp; rep from * 2 more times, sk next sc, sc in next dc, sk next sc, ***3 dc in free loop of previous back layer, sc in next dc; rep from *** across to beginning of rnd; join with sl st in top of beginning ch; sl st in next 2 dc and in first ch-3 sp. Enlarge loop on hook and keep this loop in back while working the next round. Do **not** fasten off.

Rnd 4 (front layer): Rep Rnd 3 (front layer).

Rnds 5–37: Rep Rnd 4 (both layers), changing colors as in Color Sequence.

Note: In the final rnd, unless instructed to work through both layers, all other stitches are worked in the front layer of the previous round.

Rnd 38 (only layer, back layer): Change to smaller hook, place loop of A back on hook, (sl st, ch 1, sc) in next dc of front layer, 2 sc in next tr and corresponding ch-3 sp, *sc in next dc, sc in next sc, sc in next ch-1 sp, 3 sc in next dc, sc in next ch-1 sp, sc in next sc, **sl st in next sl st, sc in next sc, sc in next ch-1 sp, 3 sc in next dc, sc in next ch-1 sp, sc in next sc; rep from ** across to next corner, sc in next dc, 2 sc in next tr and corresponding ch-3 sp; rep from * 2 more times, sc in next dc, sc in next sc, sc in next ch-1 sp, 3 sc in next dc, sc in next ch-1 sp, sc in next sc, ***sl st in next sl st, sc in next sc, sc in next ch-1 sp, 3 sc in next dc, sc in next ch-1 sp, sc in next sc; rep from ** across to beginning of rnd; join with sl st in first sc. Fasten off.

FINISHING
Using yarn needle, weave in all ends.

funky granny wrap

 EASY

designed by Edie Eckman

FINISHED MEASUREMENTS
Width   16"/40.5cm
Length   52"/132cm

MATERIALS

Caron International's Simply Soft **MEDIUM 4**
(100% acrylic; 6 oz/170g, 315 yds/288m):
#9761 Plum Perfect, 9 oz (A)
#9759 Ocean, 6 oz (B)
#9754 Persimmon, 6 oz (C)
#9755 Sunshine, 6 oz (D)
#9757 Wine Country, 6 oz (E)

Crochet hook, one size US I/9 (5.5mm), or size to obtain gauge
Yarn needle

GAUGE
One Funky Granny Square = 4" x 4"/10 x 10cm.
Gauge is not critical for this project.

ABBREVIATIONS
rep	repeat
rnd(s)	round(s)
RS	right side
sk	skip
sp(s)	space(s)
st	stitch

SPECIAL TERMS

FPdc: Front-post double crochet—Yarn over, insert hook from front to back and then to front again around post of stitch, yarn over and draw up loop, [yarn over and draw through 2 loops on hook] twice.

Joining chain: Ch 1, sl st in corresponding ch-sp of neighboring square, ch 1.

STITCHES USED

Chain (ch)
Double crochet (dc)
Single crochet (sc)
Slip stitch (sl st)

NOTES

1. The first three rounds of each square are worked with B, C, D, or E. Then Rnds 4 and 5 are worked with A.
2. Squares are joined to previous squares while working Rnd 5.
3. Work granny squares with RS facing throughout.

FIRST FUNKY GRANNY SQUARE

Note: First granny square appears in upper left corner of assembly diagram.

With B, ch 4; join with sl st in first ch to form a ring.

Rnd 1 (RS): Ch 1, 8 sc in ring; join with sl st in first sc—8 sc.

Rnd 2: Ch 5 (counts as dc, ch 2), *dc in next sc, ch 2; rep from * around; join with sl st in 3rd ch of beginning ch—8 dc and 8 ch-2 sps.

Rnd 3: Ch 1, sc in same st as join, (dc, [ch 1, dc] 6 times) in next dc (corner made), *sc in next dc, (dc, [ch 1, dc] 6 times) in next dc (corner made); rep from * around; join with sl st in first sc—4 corners and 4 sc. Fasten off.

Rnd 4: With RS facing, join A with sc in last dc of any corner group, working in front of next sc, FPdc around post of next dc in Rnd 2, sc in next dc, * [ch 3, sk (ch 1, dc), sc in next ch-sp, ch 3, sk (dc, ch 1), sc in next dc] 2 times, working in front of next sc, FPdc around post of next dc in Rnd 2, sc in next dc; rep from * 2 more times, ch 3, sk (ch 1, dc), sc in next ch-sp, ch 3, sk (dc, ch 1), sc in next dc, ch 3, sk (ch 1, dc), sc in next ch-2 sp; join with dc in first sc (join counts as ch-3 sp)—16 ch-3 sps, 4 FPdc, and 20 sc.

Rnd 5: Ch 1, sc in first ch-3 sp (formed by join), [ch 3, sc in next ch-sp] 2 times, ch 3, (dc, ch 3, dc) in next sc, *[ch 3, sc in next ch-sp] 4 times, ch 3, (dc, ch 3, dc) in next sc; rep from * 2 more times, ch 3, sc in next ch-sp, ch 3; join with sl st in first sc—24 ch-3 sps. Fasten off.

funky granny wrap chart

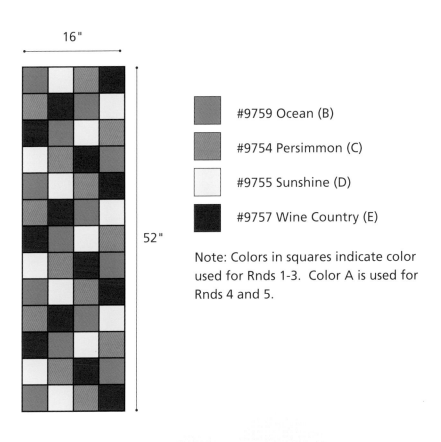

16"

52"

#9759 Ocean (B)

#9754 Persimmon (C)

#9755 Sunshine (D)

#9757 Wine Country (E)

Note: Colors in squares indicate color used for Rnds 1-3. Color A is used for Rnds 4 and 5.

NEXT FUNKY GRANNY SQUARE
(make and join 51)

Note: Refer to assembly diagram for color and placement of each square. Work as for first granny square through Rnd 4.

Each granny square is now joined to previous one or two granny squares (refer to assembly diagram). Work the appropriate joining round, based on whether the square needs to be joined to previous square(s) across one edge or two edges. Review instructions for joining chain (page 10) before beginning Rnd 5.

Rnd 5 (one-edge joining rnd): Ch 1, sc in first ch-3 sp (formed by join), [ch 3, sc in next ch-sp] 2 times, *ch 3, (dc, ch 3, dc) in next sc, [ch 3, sc in next ch-sp] 4 times; rep from * one more time, ch 3, dc in next corner sc, work joining chain in corresponding corner ch-sp of neighboring square, dc in same corner sc (corner join made), [work joining chain in corresponding ch-sp of neighboring square, sc in next ch-sp of current square] 4 times, work joining chain in corresponding ch-sp of neighboring square, dc in next corner sc, work joining chain in corresponding corner ch-sp of neighboring square, dc in same corner sc (corner join made), ch 3, sc in next ch-sp of current square, ch 3; join with sl st in first sc. Fasten off.

Rnd 5 (two-edge joining rnd): Ch 1, sc in first ch-3 sp (formed by join), [ch 3, sc in next ch-sp] 2 times, ch 3, (dc, ch 3, dc) in next sc, [ch 3, sc in next ch-sp] 4 times, ch 3, dc in next corner sc, work joining chain in corresponding corner ch-sp of neighboring square, dc in same corner sc (corner join made), *[work joining chain in corresponding ch-sp of neighboring square, sc in next ch-sp of current square] 4 times, work joining chain in corresponding ch-sp of neighboring square, dc in next corner sc, work joining chain in corresponding corner ch-sp of neighboring square, dc in same corner sc (corner join made); rep from * once more, ch 3, sc in next ch-sp of current square, ch 3; join with sl st in first sc. Fasten off.

Note: To join a square into a corner formed by three squares, join square in the corner space of only one of the neighboring squares.

FINISHING
Using yarn needle, weave in all ends. Block wrap, if desired.

granny on the corner

Shown on page 15.

designed by Kimberley Biddix

 EASY

FINISHED MEASUREMENTS
Width 36"/91.5cm, including border
Length 62"/157.5cm, including border

MATERIALS
Caron International's Simply Soft **MEDIUM 4**
(100% acrylic; 6 oz/170g, 315 yds/288m):
#9707 Dark Sage, 6 oz (A)
#9750 Chocolate, 12 oz (B)
Caron International's Simply Soft Heather
(100% acrylic; 5 oz/141.8g, 250 yds/228m):
#9503 Woodland Heather, 10 oz (C)
#9502 Truffle Heather, 10 oz (D)

Crochet hook, size US H/8 (5mm), or size to obtain gauge
Yarn needle

GAUGE
One square = $6^1/_4$" x $6^1/_4$"/16 x 16cm
Gauge is not critical for this project.

ABBREVIATIONS
rep	repeat
rnd	round
RS	right side
sp(s)	space(s)
st(s)	stitch(es)
WS	wrong side

SPECIAL TERM

dc2tog: Double crochet 2 together—
[Yarn over, insert hook in next st and
draw up a loop, yarn over and draw
through 2 loops] twice, yarn over and
draw through all 3 loops on hook.

STITCHES USED

Chain (ch)
Double crochet (dc)
Half double crochet (hdc)
Single crochet (sc)
Slip stitch (sl st)

SQUARE (make 45)

With C, ch 4.

Rnd 1 (RS): Work 15 dc in 4th ch from
hook (beginning ch counts as first
dc); join with sl st in top of beginning
ch—16 dc.

Rnd 2: Ch 4 (counts as dc, ch 1), [dc
in next dc, ch 1] 15 times; join with
sl st in 3rd ch of beginning ch—16 dc
and 16 ch-1 sps.

Rnd 3: Sl st in first ch-1 sp, ch 3
(counts as first dc here and
throughout), (dc, ch 2, 2 dc) in same
ch-1 sp (corner made), *ch 1, hdc in
next ch-1 sp, ch 1, sc in next ch-1 sp,
ch 1, hdc in next ch-1 sp, ch 1, (2 dc,
ch 2, 2 dc) in next ch-1 sp (corner
made); rep from * 2 more times,
ch 1, hdc in next ch-1 sp, ch 1, sc
in next ch-1 sp, ch 1, hdc in next
ch-1 sp, ch 1; join with sl st in top of
beginning ch—4 corners, 8 hdc, 4 sc,
and 16 ch-1 sps. Fasten off C.

Work now proceeds back and forth in
rows across two sides only of square.

Row 4: With RS facing, join A with
sl st in any corner ch-2 sp, ch 3, dc
in same ch-2 sp, [ch 1, dc in next
ch-1 sp] 4 times, ch 1, (2 dc, ch 2,
2 dc) in next corner ch-2 sp, [ch 1, dc
in next ch-1 sp] 4 times, ch 1, 2 dc
in next corner ch-2 sp, turn; leave
remaining sts unworked—1 corner,
12 dc (6 dc on each side), and
10 ch-1 sps (5 ch-1 sps on each side).

Row 5: Ch 3, 2 dc in each ch-1 sp
across to corner ch-2 sp, (2 dc, ch 2,
2 dc) in corner ch-2 sp, 2 dc in each
ch-1 sp across other side, dc in top of
turning ch—1 corner, and ten 2-dc
groups (five 2-dc groups on each
side), and 1 dc at each end. Fasten
off A.

Row 6: With RS facing, join D with
sl st in first dc, ch 3, dc in same dc,
*2 dc in sp between next two 2-dc
groups; rep from * across to corner
ch-2 sp, (2 dc, ch 2, 2 dc) in corner
ch-2 sp, **2 dc in sp between next
two 2-dc groups; rep from ** across,
2 dc in sp between last 2-dc group
and turning ch, turn—1 corner, and
twelve 2-dc groups (six 2-dc groups
on each side).

Row 9: Ch 1, sc in each dc to corner ch-2 sp, 3 sc in corner ch-2 sp, sc in each dc across, sc in top of turning ch—37 sc. Fasten off.

FINISHING
Arrange squares as shown in assembly diagram. Sew squares together.

Border
With RS facing, join B in any corner of afghan.

Rnd 1: Ch 3, dc in each sc around, working dc2tog over 2 sc at each inside corner (where squares meet) and 3 dc in each outside corner, around; join with sl st in top of beginning ch. Fasten off.

Using yarn needle, weave in all ends.

Row 7: Ch 3, *2 dc in sp between next two 2-dc groups; rep from * across to corner ch-2 sp, (2 dc, ch 2, 2 dc) in corner ch-2 sp, **2 dc in sp between next two 2-dc groups; rep from ** across, dc in top of turning ch—1 corner, twelve 2-dc groups (six 2-dc groups on each side), and 1 dc at each end. Fasten off D.

Fringe
Cut strands of all colors 16"/40.5cm long. Holding 2 strands of each color together, fold fringe in half, and attach to each point across both short ends, as follows: * Using crochet hook, insert hook from WS to RS into point, pull fold through forming a loop, insert ends into loop and pull tight against edge; rep from * across all points of both short ends. Trim ends of fringe.

Row 8: With RS facing, join B with sl st in first st, ch 3, dc in each dc across to corner ch-2 sp, (2 dc, ch 2, 2 dc) in corner ch-2 sp, dc in each dc across, dc in top of turning ch, turn—1 corner and 30 dc (15 dc on each side).

granny on the corner chart

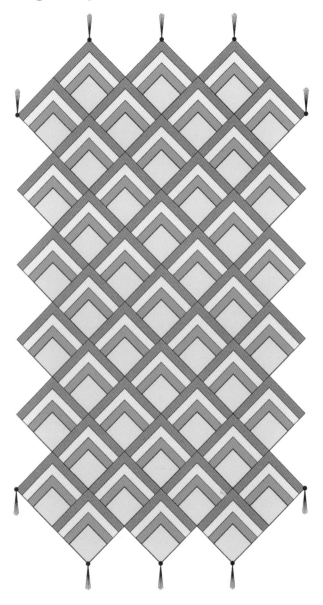

 #9707 Dark Sage (A)

#9750 Chocolate (B)

#9503 Woodland Heather (C)

#9502 Truffle Heather (D)

● Fringe

christmas granny

 EASY

designed by Kim Guzman

FINISHED MEASUREMENTS
Width   45"/114.5cm
Length   52"/132cm

MATERIALS
Caron International's Simply Soft
(100% acrylic; 6 oz/170g, 315 yds/288m):
#9757 Wine Country, 12 oz (A)
#9760 Pine, 18 oz (B)
Caron International's Simply Soft Heather
(100% acrylic; 5 oz/141.8g, 250 yds/228m):
#9503 Woodland Heather, 25 oz (C)

Crochet hooks, one each size US I/9 (5.5mm) (for squares), US K/10.5
(6.5mm) (for finishing), or size to obtain gauge.
Yarn needle

GAUGE
Rnd 1 = approx 1¹/₂" x 1¹/₂"/4 x 4cm;
Square = 7¹/₄" x 7¹/₄"/18.5 x 18.5cm, worked with smaller hook.
Gauge is not critical for this project.

ABBREVIATIONS
rep   repeat
rnd   round
RS   right side
sk   skip
sp(s)   space(s)
st(s)   stitch(es)
WS   wrong side

STITCHES USED

Chain (ch)
Double crochet (dc)
Half double crochet (hdc)
Single crochet (sc)
Slip stitch (sl st)
Treble crochet (tr)

NOTE

Weave in ends as work progresses.

SQUARE (make 42)

With smaller hook and A, ch 4; join with sl st in first ch to form a ring.

Rnd 1 (RS): Ch 3 (counts as dc here and throughout), work 15 dc in ring; join with sl st in top of beginning ch—16 dc.

Rnd 2: *Ch 8, sc in 4th ch from hook, hdc in next ch, dc in next ch, tr in next ch, dc in next ch (petal made), sk next dc of Rnd 1, sl st in next dc; rep from * 6 more times, ch 8, sc in 4th ch from hook, hdc in next ch, dc in next ch, tr in next ch, dc in next ch, sk next dc of Rnd 1; join with sl st in top of beginning ch of Rnd 1—8 petals. Fasten off A.

Rnd 3: With RS facing, join B with sc in any ch-3 sp (at tip of a petal), ch 2, sc in same ch-3 sp, *sc in next 5 sts (down side of petal), ch 7, sl st in 7th ch from hook, sk next sl st (between petals), working in free loops along opposite side of foundation ch of next petal, sc in next 5 sts, (sc, ch 2, sc) in next ch-3 sp (at tip of petal), sc in next 5 sts (down side of petal), ch 5, sl st in 5th ch from hook, sk next sl st (between petals), working in free loops along opposite side of foundation ch of next petal, sc in next 5 sts, (sc, ch 2, sc) in next ch-3 sp (at tip of petal); rep from * 2 more times, sc in next 5 sts (down side of petal), ch 7, sl st in 7th ch from hook, sk next sl st (between petals), working in free loops along opposite side of foundation ch of next petal, sc in next 5 sts, (sc, ch 2, sc) in next ch-3 sp (at tip of petal), sc in next 5 sts (down side of petal), ch 5, sl st in 5th ch from hook, sk next sl st (between petals), working in free loops along opposite side of foundation ch of next petal, sc in next 5 sts; join with sl st in first sc. Fasten off B.

Rnd 4: With RS facing, join C with sl st in any ch-7 sp (between petals), ch 4, (2 tr, ch 3, 3 tr) in same ch-7 sp, *sc in next ch-2 sp (at tip of petal), 5 tr in next ch-5 sp, sc in next ch-2 sp, (3 tr, ch 3, 3 tr) in next ch-7 sp; rep from * 2 more times, sc in next ch-2 sp, 5 tr in next ch-5 sp, sc in next ch-2 sp; join with sl st in top of beginning ch.

Rnd 5: Ch 3, dc in next 2 sts, *(3 dc, ch 2, 3 dc) in next ch-3 sp, dc in next 13 sts; rep from * 2 more times, (3 dc, ch 2, 3 dc) in next ch-3 sp, dc in next 10 sts; join with sl st in top of beginning ch. Fasten off C.

Rnd 6: With RS facing, join B with sl st in any ch-2 sp, ch 1, *3 sc in same ch-2 sp, sc in each st across to next ch-2 sp; rep from * around; join with sl st in first sc. Fasten off B.

STRIP (make 6)

With yarn needle and B, sew seven squares into a strip. With RS facing and smaller hook, join B with sl st in center sc of any corner of strip, ch 1, work 3 sc in same sc, work 147 sc evenly spaced across each long side, 21 sc across each short side, and 3 sc in center sc of each corner; join with sl st in first sc. Fasten off B. Rep to make 6 strips.

FINISHING
Join Strips

With WS facing each other, join two strips across long edges as follows: With larger hook and 2 strands of C held together, join yarn with sl st in center sc of corner of one strip to work across a long side, ch 1, sl st in corresponding sc of 2nd strip, *ch 1, sl st in next sc of first strip, ch 1, sl st in next sc of 2nd strip; rep from * across long side edge. Fasten off C. Rep joining 4 more times to join all strips.

Border

With RS facing, larger hook and 2 strands of C held together, join yarn with sc in any corner of afghan, *ch 1, sk next st, sc in next st; rep from * around; join with sl st in first sc. Fasten off.

Using yarn needle, weave in all ends.

grannies gone wild afghan

■□□ EASY

designed by Diane Moyer

FINISHED MEASUREMENTS
Width   54"/137cm
Length   64"/162.5cm

MATERIALS
Caron International's Simply Soft
(100% acrylic; 6 oz/170g, 315 yds/288m):
#9727 Black, 48 oz (A)
#9756 Lavender Blue, 6 oz (B)
#9755 Sunshine, 6 oz (C)
#9742 Grey Heather, 6 oz (D)
#9754 Persimmon, 6 oz (E)
Caron International's Simply Soft Brites
(100% acrylic; 6 oz/170g, 315 yds/288m):
#9611 Rose Violet, 6 oz (F)
#9608 Blue Mint, 6 oz (G)

Crochet hook, size US I/9 (5.5mm), or size to obtain gauge
Pins
Yarn needle

GAUGE
Large Square = 7" x 7"/18 x 18cm;
Small Square = 3^1/$_2$" x 3^1/$_2$"/9 x 9cm.
Gauge is not critical for this project.

ABBREVIATIONS

rep   repeat
rnd(s)   round(s)
RS   right side
sk   skip
sp(s)   space(s)
st   stitch

STITCHES USED

Chain (ch)
Double crochet (dc)
Single crochet (sc)
Slip stitch (sl st)

NOTES

1. All squares are made separately and then joined with a lacy joining pattern.
2. When fastening off, leave a 4–6"/10–15cm tail to weave in later. Whenever possible, work over ends to eliminate weaving them in later.
3. Always work with **right** side facing.
4. The color combinations given in the assembly diagram can be followed or you may use colors as desired, making the number of squares required, and arranging them according to the assembly diagram.

HELPFUL TIP

When assembling the afghan, you may prefer using a hook slightly smaller than the one used to make the squares. Pinning squares to be seamed is helpful. Be sure to match seams when assembling the larger pieces.

LARGE SQUARE (make 30)

Note: Make the squares in the color combinations indicated on the assembly diagram, or as desired.

With first color and larger hook, ch 4; join with sl st in first ch to form a ring.

Rnd 1 (RS): Ch 3 (counts as dc here and throughout), 2 dc in ring, ch 2, [3 dc in ring, ch 2] 3 times; join with sl st in top of beginning ch—Four 3-dc groups and 4 ch-2 sps. Fasten off.

Rnd 2: With RS facing, join A with sl st in any ch-2 sp, ch 4 (counts as sc, ch 3 here and throughout), sc in same ch-2 sp, [ch 3, (sc, ch 3, sc) in next ch-2 sp] 3 times, ch 3; join with sl st in first ch of beginning ch—8 sc and 8 ch-3 sps.

Rnd 3: Sl st in first ch-3 sp, ch 3, (2 dc, ch 3, 3 dc) in same ch-3 sp (corner made), ch 1, 3 dc in next ch-3 sp, ch 1, [(3 dc, ch 3, 3 dc) in next ch-3 sp (corner made), ch 1, 3 dc in next ch-3 sp, ch 1] 3 times; join with sl st in top of beginning ch—4 corners, 12 dc (one 3-dc group on each side), and 8 ch-1 sps (two ch-1 sps on each side). Fasten off.

Rnd 4: With RS facing, join 2nd color with sl st in any corner ch-3 sp, ch 4, sc in same ch-3 sp, [ch 3, *sc in next ch-1 sp, ch 3; rep from * to next corner ch-3 sp, (sc, ch 3, sc) in corner ch-3 sp] 3 times, ch 3, **sc in next ch-1 sp, ch 3; rep from ** around; join with sl st in first ch of beginning ch—16 sc and 16 ch-3 sps.

Rnd 5: Sl st in first ch-3 sp, ch 3, (2 dc, ch 3, 3 dc) in same ch-3 sp, [ch 1, *3 dc in next ch-3 sp, ch 1; rep from * to next corner ch-3 sp, (3 dc, ch 3, 3 dc) in corner ch-3 sp] 3 times, ch 1, **3 dc in next ch-3 sp, ch 1; rep from ** around; join with sl st in top of beginning ch—4 corners, 36 dc (three 3-dc groups on each side), and 16 ch-1 sps (four ch-1 sps on each side). Fasten off.

Rnds 6 and 7: With first color, rep Rnds 4 and 5. Fasten off.

Rnd 8: With A, rep Rnd 4.

Rnd 9: Ch 1, sc in same st as join, work 1 sc in each sc, 3 sc in each non-corner ch-3 sp, and 5 sc in each corner ch-3 sp around; join with sl st in first sc. Fasten off.

SMALL TWO-COLORED SQUARE
(make 75)
Note: Make the squares in the color combinations indicated on the assembly diagram, or as desired.

With first color and larger hook, ch 4; join with sl st in first ch to form a ring.

Rnd 1 (RS): Work Rnd 1 of large square. Fasten off.

Rnds 2 and 3: With second color, work Rnds 2 and 3 of large square. Fasten off.

Rnd 4: With RS facing, join A with sl st in any corner ch-3 sp, ch 1, work 1 sc in each dc and ch-1 sp, and 5 sc in each corner ch-3 sp around; join with sl st in first sc. Fasten off.

SMALL SOLID SQUARE (make 75)
With A and larger hook, ch 4; join with sl st in first ch to form a ring.

Rnd 1 (RS): Work Rnd 1 of large square. Do not fasten off.

Rnd 2: Sl st in first ch-2 sp, ch 4, sc in same ch-2 sp, [ch 3, (sc, ch 3, sc) in next ch-2 sp] 3 times, ch 3; join with sl st in first ch of beginning ch—8 sc and 8 ch-3 sps. Do not fasten off.

Rnd 3: Work Rnd 3 of large square. Do **not** fasten off.

Rnd 4: Ch 1, sc in same st as join, work 1 sc in each dc and ch-1 sp, and 5 sc in each corner ch-3 sp around; join with sl st in first sc. Fasten off.

FINISHING
Using yarn needle, weave in all ends. Block squares. Arrange squares according to assembly diagram.

Seam Squares

With RS of two neighboring squares together, working through both thicknesses, join A with sl st in center sc of first 5-sc corner, *ch 1, sk next sc of both squares, sl st in next sc; rep from * across edge, ending seam with sl st in center sc of next 5-sc corner. If necessary, do not skip a sc to end the seam evenly; do not (ch 1, sk next sc), instead eliminate the ch-1, and sl st into the next sc. When seaming pieces containing seams, take care to match seams and to work a sc into all seams.

Note: Seam five small squares to each large square first, then seam these larger squares into strips, and finally seam the strips together.

Edging

Rnd 1: With RS facing, join A with sl st in first sc of any corner, ch 4, sc in 5th sc of corner, ch 3, *sk next 3 sc, sc in next sc, ch 3; rep from * to next corner, [sc in first sc of corner, ch 3, sc in 5th sc of corner, ch 3, **sk next 3 sc, sc in next sc, ch 3; rep from ** to next corner] 3 times; join with sl st in first ch of beginning ch.

Note: When reaching an area where two squares are joined, sc in corner of the first square, ch 3, sc in corner of second square (skipping the seam).

Rnd 2: Sl st in first ch-sp, ch 3, (2 dc, ch 3, 3 dc) in same ch-sp, ch 1, *3 dc in next ch-3 sp, ch 1; rep from * to next corner ch-3 sp, [(3 dc, ch 3, 3 dc) in corner ch-3 sp, ch 1, **3 dc in next ch-3 sp, ch 1; rep from ** to next corner ch-3 sp] 3 times; join with sl st in top of beginning ch.

Rnd 3: Sl st in each st to first corner ch-sp, (sl st, ch 4, sc) in corner ch-sp, ch 3, sk next 3 dc, *sc in next ch-1 sp, ch 3, sk next 3 dc; rep from * to next corner, [(sc, ch 3, sc) in corner ch-sp, ch 3, sk next 3 dc, **sc in next ch-1 sp, ch 3, sk next 3 dc; rep from ** to next corner] 3 times; join with sl st in first ch of beginning ch.

Rnd 4: Rep Rnd 2. Fasten off.

Using yarn needle, weave in all ends.

grannies gone wild chart

Row 1

G/C	A	D/E			A		G/F	A	D/C			A		B/F	A			A	D/B	A	C/F
	G/F				D/B		E/G		A			B/D			C/E		
F/D	A			A	D/E	A		E/F	A	C/E	A		C/E	A			A	D/G
E/C						

Row 2

A	B/D	A	C/F			A	E/B	A	F/G			A	G/E	A
E/F		B/D	A	F/G		A	F/E	E/C	
	E/C	A	B/C	A	G/E	A	C/B	F/B	A	C/D	A	D/F

Row 3

G/B	A	C/D		A	E/F	A	B/G		A	C/E	A	B/F
C/F	F/G	A	D/B	A	F/C	G/D
B/G	A	D/E	A	B/G	B/E	A	G/F	A	G/D

Row 4

A	F/E	A	D/F	A	F/C	A	E/G	A	C/G	A
B/D	E/D	C/G	C/D	G/B
G/B	A	E/B	A	B/C	F/B	A	D/F	A	B/D	D/E

Row 5

F/B	A	F/E	A	E/D	A	B/C	A	E/D	A	G/C
C/G	D/G	A	B/F	A	E/F	C/B	F/C
E/G	A	D/B	A	G/C	G/B	A	G/D	A	B/E

Row 6

A	D/F	A	F/C	A	F/E	A	D/C	A	B/G	A
F/G	E/B	G/D	G/E	G/E
B/E	C/D	A	C/G	A	B/C	F/D	A	C/B	D/C

(dimensions noted at right and bottom: 3½", 7")

#9727 BLACK (A)
#9756 LAVENDER BLUE (B)
#9755 SUNSHINE (C)
#9742 GREY HEATHER (D)
#9754 PERSIMMON (E)
#9611 ROSE VIOLET (F)
#9608 BLUE MINT (G)

In each square, the first letter indicates the first color, and the second letter indicates the second color. If only one letter is given, this is a solid color square.

deep sea granny

◼◼☐☐ EASY　　　　　　　　　*designed by Martha Brooks Stein*

FINISHED MEASUREMENTS
Width　42"/106.5cm, including border
Length　50"/127cm, including border

MATERIALS
Caron International's Simply Soft **MEDIUM 4**
(100% acrylic; 6 oz/170g, 315 yds/288m):
#9759 Ocean, 22$^1/_2$ oz (A)
#9705 Sage, 5 oz (B)
#9707 Dark Sage, 5 oz (C)
#9756 Lavender Blue, 4$^1/_2$ oz (D)
#9761 Plum Perfect, 5 oz (E)
#9709 Light Country Blue, 5 oz (F)
#9710 Country Blue, 5 oz (G)

Crochet hooks, one each size US H/8 (5mm) (for border only) and US I/9 (5.5mm), or size to obtain gauge
Yarn needle

GAUGE
One square = 3$^3/_4$" x 3$^3/_4$"/9.5 x 9.5cm
Gauge is not critical for this project.

ABBREVIATIONS

rep — repeat
rnd(s) — round(s)
RS — right side
sk — skip
sp(s) — space(s)

STITCHES USED

Chain (ch)
Double crochet (dc)
Half double crochet (hdc)
Single crochet (sc)
Slip stitch (sl st)

NOTE

The first three rounds of each square are worked with B, C, D, E, F, or G. Then the last round is worked with A.

SQUARE (make 143 – 24 with B, 24 with C, 23 with D, 24 with E, 24 with F, and 24 with G)

With larger hook, ch 4; join with sl st in first ch to form a ring.

Rnd 1 (RS): Ch 2 (counts as first dc here and throughout), 2 dc in ring, [ch 2, 3 dc in ring] 3 times; join with hdc in top of beginning ch-2 (joining hdc serves as a ch-2 sp)—12 dc (consisting of four 3-dc groups) and 4 ch-2 sps.

Rnd 2: Ch 2, 2 dc in first ch-2 sp (formed by joining hdc), [ch 1, (3 dc, ch 2, 3 dc) in next ch-2 sp] 3 times, ch 1, 3 dc in first ch-2 sp; join with hdc in top of beginning ch-2—24 dc, 4 ch-2 sps, and 4 ch-1 sps.

Rnd 3: Ch 2, 2 dc in first ch-2 sp (formed by joining hdc), [ch 1, 3 dc in next ch-1 sp, ch 1, (3 dc, ch 2, 3 dc) in next ch-2 sp] 3 times, ch 1, 3 dc in next ch-1 sp, ch 1, 3 dc in first ch-2 sp, ch 2; join with sl st in top of beginning ch-2—36 dc, 4 ch-2 sps, and 8 ch-1 sps. Fasten off.

Rnd 4: With RS facing, join A with sl st in corner ch-2 sp opposite join of Rnd 3, ch 1, sc in same corner ch-2 sp, *[ch 1, sc in center dc of next 3-dc group, ch 1, sc in next ch-sp] twice, ch 1, sc in center dc of next 3-dc group, ch 1, (sc, ch 2, sc) in corner ch-2 sp; rep from * 2 more times, [ch 1, sc in center dc of next 3-dc group, ch 1, sc in next ch-sp] twice, ch 1, sc in center dc of next 3-dc group, ch 1, sc in first ch-2 sp, ch 2; join with sl st in top of beginning sc—28 sc, 4 ch-2 sps, and 24 ch-1 sps.

Fasten off leaving a 10"/25.5cm tail for sewing squares together.

deep sea granny chart

42"

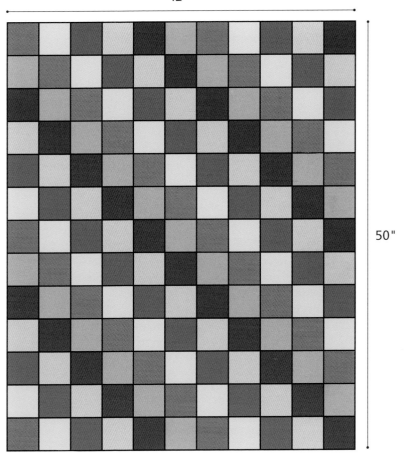

50"

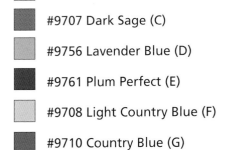

#9705 Sage (B)

#9707 Dark Sage (C)

#9756 Lavender Blue (D)

#9761 Plum Perfect (E)

#9708 Light Country Blue (F)

#9710 Country Blue (G)

Note: Colors in squares indicate color used for Rnds 1-3. Color A is used for Rnd 4.

FINISHING

Arrange squares as shown in assembly diagram. Hold neighboring squares with RS of squares together. Using yarn needle and A, whipstitch the neighboring edges together, sewing through the back loops only. Fasten off.

Border

Rnd 1: With RS facing and smaller hook, join A with sc in any corner ch-2 sp of blanket, [ch 1, *sc in next ch-sp, ch 1; rep from * across to next corner ch-2 sp of blanket, (sc, ch 2, sc) in corner ch-2 sp] 3 times, ch 1, **sc in next ch-sp, ch 1; rep from ** across to first corner ch-2 sp of blanket, sc in first ch-2 sp; join with hdc in first sc.

Rnd 2: Ch 5 (counts as dc, ch 3), dc in first ch-2 sp (formed by joining hdc), [(dc, ch 2, dc) in each ch-sp across to next corner ch-2 sp, (dc, ch 3, dc, ch 3, dc) in corner ch-2 sp] 3 times, (dc, ch 2, dc) in each ch-sp across to first corner ch-2 sp, dc in first ch-2 sp, ch 3; join with sl st in 2nd ch of beginning ch-5.

Rnds 3 and 4: Sl st in first ch-sp, ch 6 (counts as dc, ch 4), dc in same ch-sp, [(dc, ch 2, dc) in each ch-sp across to next 2 corner ch-sps, (dc, ch 4, dc) in next 2 corner ch-sps] 3 times, (dc, ch 2, dc) in each ch-sp across to next corner ch-sp, (dc, ch 4, dc) in next corner ch-sp; join with sl st in 2nd ch of beginning ch-6.
Fasten off.

Using yarn needle, weave in all ends.